Daniel M. Berg

Hard Faith

A true story

edited by Daniel York

Copyright ©2006 by Daniel M. Berg and **First Cause**.

Hard Faith
by Daniel M. Berg

Printed in the United States of America

ISBN 1-60034-597-2

All rights reserved solely by the author. The author guarantees all contents are original and do not infringe upon the legal rights of any other person or work. No part of this book may be reproduced, stored in a retrieval system, or transmitted in any form or by any means (electronic, mechanical, photocopy, recording or by any other means), except for brief quotations without prior permission in writing by the author. The views expressed in this book are not necessarily those of the publisher.

Unless otherwise indicated, Bible quotations are taken from the **New Living Translation** ©1996, 2004 Tyndale House Publishers, Inc. Wheaton, Illinois.

www.xulonpress.com

Acknowledgement

For non-believers to the most serious Christians, **Hard Faith** is a "must read experience" for anyone questioning God's faithfulness or who has doubts about the value of faith. As a friend of the Berg family, it has been an incredible blessing to be a witness to God's loving miracles that continue to be an example for us all through their life, ministry and their story as told in this book.

—Dana Hersom
Family Friend and CEO idataGATE Corporation

Having had the pleasure of meeting Dan and Doris after the events of this time in their lives and not knowing anything about their past, **Hard Faith** pierced my heart and brought me to my knees. To know Dan and Doris now one would never guess they ever dealt with such painful issues. I thank God for allowing our paths to cross and using their story to strengthen my relationship with Him.

Thank you both for showing all who read this book the unmistakable power and love of Our Lord and Savior Jesus Christ!

"**Each time He said, 'My grace is all you need. My power works best in weakness.'**"
—2 Corinthians 12:9

—Ann Marie Garner
Loving Friend

Dedication

This book is dedicated to my loving children
Gabriel and Nicole
and to my beloved wife and best friend,
Doris.

Introduction

Growing up I was never satisfied with my testimony. I always thought because I was a pastor's child and I grew up in church that there was no way for me to have a gripping testimony to share with those that were hurting. My life seemed pretty normal to me. Not having Mom around often was not so unusual; Dad worked hard and going to the babysitter was part of everyday life. Now that I am nineteen years old and look back on that "normal" life I have seen that God's hand never left my father's side, things were rough and I had absolutely no idea.

For about four months every Sunday, Dad went into his office at home and wrote as the Lord led him. He was telling his story; a story that I never considered until now, a story whose hiding was best for all of us. It was safest for him to keep it to himself then the possibility of rejection by others was not a problem. But staying safe is not always what God has in mind! He can use this story and I believe He will to minister to many people of all walks of life. So this is a true story from a family whose struggles and victory hopefully will help so many others whose lives today are challenged.

That testimony that I was so concerned about is no longer a worry. My parents have shown me that God can use whoever He wants and in whatever way He wants. My Mom is just about one of the sweetest women you can meet and My dad is one of the strongest men I know because he stuck with my mom when she needed him the most and that only happened by the grace and mercy of our Heavenly Father.

Nicole Berg
Daughter

CONTENTS

Forward xiii
Chapter 1:   White Picket Fences 17
Chapter 2:   The Weather of a Wedding 21
Chapter 3:   The Marriage Bed of Glass 25
Chapter 4:   Above the Clouds 27
Chapter 5:   House of Cards 31
Chapter 6:   "Get Your Own Door Jam!" 37
Chapter 7:   Why? 43
Chapter 8:   "Check Out This Toolbox!" 49
Chapter 9:   Rules of the Game 53
Chapter 10: "Just Fall!" 59
Chapter 11: Pulling Teeth 63
Chapter 12: "Go to Hell!" 69
Chapter 13: Everyone is Driving My Car 75
Chapter 14: Off Sides 79
Chapter 15: Off Route 87
Chapter 16: Time 95
Chapter 17: Choosing Miracles 99
Chapter 18: Paper Ham 105
Hard Faith 111

Forward

Daily, difficult choices in our marriage equal or surpass battlefield heroics.

During wartime, rugged physical training, deprivation of civilian comfort, sacrifice of all kinds, including casualties of wounded and killed are expected and stoically accepted. This is all part of the price of pain and suffering that must be paid for victory and an enduring peace.

In WWII, as part of the so-called Greatest Generation, I was a young man in my late teens and early twenties. As a result of three battles in the Pacific, the last one being Okinawa, I spent eighteen months in various Naval hospitals, having been shot through the neck and hand by a Japanese sniper.

I eventually ended up for one year in the Philadelphia Naval Hospital, a giant medical complex overflowing with young Marine and Navy casualties from the battles on and offshore of Iwo Jima, Okinawa and other parts of the Pacific. These thousands of casualties were expected and reluctantly accepted by a grieving, but grateful nation.

But there is another kind of suffering that is much more difficult to describe and accept. This type of tribulation is certainly often impossible to define in words. It is the mysterious pain and indescribable agony of the inner heart—both in an individual and in a family.

Who can see or understand the heart-anguish of a young, newly widowed woman whose husband is a war casualty? Or the indescribable pain of a divorce or breakup of a deep, loving relationship that refuses to heal even with the passing of time? And what about the perpetual agony of loving, praying parents for a son who is incarcerated for a lifetime without possibility of parole? There are no visible scars, no Purple Heart awarded, but these invisible wounds are often more deep and painful.

In this book, you will discover that what hardship needs is **Hard Faith**. Dan Berg does not, and probably cannot, take you to the depth of the pain and suffering he and his wife Doris endured. Yet he still shares their story in an absolutely amazing, honest and compelling manner that will cause many to relate and search their own life and marriage relationship.

The holy Scripture gives us this intrepid wisdom:

"Who among you fears the LORD and obeys the word of His servant? Let him who walks in the dark, who has no light, trust in the name of the LORD and rely on his God."
—Isaiah 50.10 (New International Version)

No one in life evades some period of darkness. The duration for some is longer than others. Dan Berg has vividly painted a word picture of his dark world that, because of his courageous honesty, will shine light and give hope to those whose lights are flickering and ready to be extinguished.

Hard Faith demands both a soft, pliable, responsive heart before the Living God and a tough forehead to resist the demands of a selfish world.

Dan and Doris's extremely difficult choices in their lives and marriage truly equal or surpass battlefield heroics.

—Robert Boardman,
WWII decorated combat Marine and author of:
A Higher Honor, Unforgettable Men in Unforgettable Times and
C-Rations For The Warrior's Heart

Chapter 1

White Picket Fences

The Bible tells us faith is hoped for but not seen.* When I used to think about marriage my hopes centered on certain images. In particular, one strong impression always stood out. Mentally, I pictured a neat, white, picket fence surrounding the house where my wife and I would live.

Neither Doris nor I came from homes with white picket fences. In Doris' case the fences were knocked down so that the wild animals could come and go as they pleased. In my case, my father's favorite color was not white, and World War II had so confused him he didn't know even where to put a fence. He would not have stayed long as he ventured from one woman to another!

It's funny in a strange way how we can grow up in a home of pain and confusion yet still have an idea of what a good home should be. My ideal home was pain and confusion-free with a white picket fence around it. But should suffering and uncertainty pop in to our lives I always believed if they were handled correctly the fence would become much stronger and brighter. This is what Doris and I have come to understand. This is our story...

Doris and I knew each other for three years before we dated. Each thought the other was stuck up (this is before we became good looking). Really, we were just shy people. Doris hid behind her hair and I hid behind my beard. As we went out with friends from church we would see each other and want to talk, but small talk is as far as it went. After a failed relationship, I told the Lord I didn't want to have another relationship with a woman. I wanted to be a eunuch and work in a salt mine. As you can see, I got a little desperate.

Then one night Doris approached me at church. I was showing people some pictures I had just taken from a trip to Yosemite and she wanted to see them. She showed an interest in nature and hiking; things that were very close to my heart. I thought, "Man, I'm on my way to a salt mine and *now* she talks to me?" (Oh, by the way, I wasn't all that crazy about becoming a eunuch).

    Doris talked to me about things I liked. What are the chances of that happening? I found out later she was just too tired of waiting for me to talk to her! Anyway, a prayer began to form in my mind that went something like this:

Lord, You know that salt mine, eunuch thing? Well, Doris has talked to me and I don't want to hurt her feelings. You wouldn't want that, would You Lord? So, if we could put that salt-mine-eunuch-thing on hold, I am going to ask her on a date. Amen.

*Hebrews 11:1

Chapter 2

The Weather Of A Wedding

When I look at what defines good memories one of the essentials is great weather. Maybe you are the same way. Doris and I went out on our first date to the mountains and the weather was great! Under blue skies and white puffy clouds, we hiked to the top of a mountain that was covered with huge rocks. I cornered her in a cave so she had no way out. (I think you can go to jail for doing that these days).

I told her that I would like to get to know her better. She returned the same thoughts to me. We dated for six months and I asked her to marry me. The first thing that came out of her mouth was laughter! Little did I know that in later years this would be the theme of our life together. As I was down on one knee and being laughed at for asking a woman to spend the rest of her life with me I realized it was pretty funny! Fortunately, she said, "Yes!"

Some lovers when telling their story will say, "We didn't have much money but we loved each other." For us we had no money and I lusted after Doris. A friend told Doris to keep a fat Bible between us, so that's what she did and I took a lot of cold showers—lots of cold showers! (There is a fine line between love and lust). Eventually, we got the money together and the wedding was scheduled. We married on June 24, 1983.

Typical with most weddings, things were coming together at the last minute. The weather was good and holding as our friends began to show up. Every one sat down and the music began to play and play and play and play. What was wrong? As I was waiting in the wings, word came back to me that Doris' family had not yet arrived.

While Doris and I were dating we talked a lot, often late into the nights. From time to time she would tell me about her early years growing up. She had a tough life, being tossed around from one family to another. Many times she was left to take care of herself. But as tough as her stories were, I knew there was much more she wasn't saying. When her family finally showed up, that hidden part of the story blew into our wedding day like dark clouds covering the true colors of a spring garden.

My first thought was "run and just keep running," (a Forest Gump type of run; not stopping until your beard is down to your waist). Just as I was looking for what window to escape through on my run for life, Doris came in and I laid my running shoes down. She was beautiful.

Unfortunately, the first time I met her family it was not a good first impression. They had not only seen hard times, it looked like "hard times" was the only thing they were on time for! As I remember that day, her family seemed to be poor, dirty, uneducated and secretive. Not only was the garden under a black cloud, weeds were beginning to appear—an omen of things to come.

Chapter 3

The Marriage Bed of Glass

Glass . . . what an invention! . . . an object to see through or to see with if you are my age! Though we enjoy its uses, we pretty much go through life not noticing it, but glass has a drawback and that is when it breaks. It cannot be repaired, only replaced. So, when we hear the sound of glass breaking we know something is gone forever. As we mourn the loss, the clean up begins shard by shard. We place the pieces in the trash as those who are looking on say, "Be careful it's sharp! Don't cut yourself!" Not until every piece is removed is it really safe to go back.

An abused person has a life broken like glass, an innocent childhood gone forever. The wedding bed to my new wife was glass that had been broken over and over again, but now it was my bed as well.

My new wife told me that night that from the age of eight years old a friend of her mother's molested her. He also used her for child pornography leading to rapes and abuse by her older brother and his friends whenever they wanted until she finally ran away at the age of seventeen. Her mother knew about all the abuse and did nothing about it! The best she could muster was the lame excuse that "everyone has problems." Doris cried all night until she fell asleep in my arms saying, " I am so sorry, I am so sorry, I am so sorry." While she was crying, the one who had protected himself his whole life from being cut, sat thinking, *"What did I just get myself into!"*

Chapter 4

Above The Clouds

Before Doris and I married I did a lot of rock climbing. Every weekend my climbing buddy and I were off early Saturday mornings. Our goal was to climb the rocks and complete the route we talked about all through the previous week. And the one thing we always hoped for was to get above the clouds on a sheer rock face. This is a place few people have seen.

As we climbed everything seemed so quiet. The only sound was our climbing gear hitting our sides. The higher we rose the more excited we grew until soon the clouds were below us and bluer than blue sky was above us. It seemed like this time could last forever, and then it happened! A slight breeze would blow against us and before long the cloud layer was gone. Below us we heard people talking and looking up at us, some thinking "your crazy!" Others wondered how in the world we got up there. Some were afraid for us—thinking we would fall. And yes, there was always the last group, those who hoped we'd fall.

For me, as someone involved in ministry, the *idea* of getting married was like climbing above the clouds. High on the rock, quiet and alone, where Doris and I could enjoy the view. Then the breezes of life blew the clouds away and suddenly we were being watched. This was okay for me but a whole different story for Doris.

I was used to being out in front of people. As long as I didn't have to look them in the face, I was ok. You see, I have some of the biggest "buck teeth" a man can have. Plus it didn't help growing up in a home where my brother told me, "You may be ugly but your personality stinks too!" Rude awakenings at a young age make you a survivor or a victim. I was a survivor but now I was about to discover firsthand what it was like to know a victim. "Numb" was the term that best tagged my new wife. I climbed with a focus towards reaching higher ground. Doris could only hear people talking below and feel their stares. She did not want to go any higher.

Early in our marriage, I began working with a high schooler named Tom. My goal was to minister to the youth in our church through working with him. I hoped that in the process we could start a youth group. Things didn't exactly progress the way I planned. We soon had a group of young people but they did not become the typical youth group. Instead, they were a conduit for reaching a group of kids I never dreamed of reaching! I met kids from broken and hurting homes just like the ones Doris and I were trying to forget! As I shared with Tom about Jesus, he in turn told his friend Lisa, and Lisa then told all her friends at her school about God's Son! God used Lisa to bring many mixed-up kids to hear the great news that there was a new life for those who would follow Jesus.

Doris and I fit in well with this group because they didn't care about our hair or teeth or where we came from, just that we were real. We hung out together and shared the life of Jesus with each other. Today many of them have special places in our hearts. Amazingly, our numbers kept expanding even as Lisa and Tom moved on, God brought others into our lives. Soon we were nearly the same size as the church, and this brought a lot of attention. For me, these were exciting times like climbing above the clouds. But the higher I went, the less I recognized that Doris' eyes were looking a different direction and hearing different voices. As I climbed for the clouds, I left her behind me, which was definitely a "bad move!"

Chapter 5

House Of Cards

As a kid I spent a lot of afternoons making houses of cards. I would go off to some place where no one was and take out a deck of playing cards. I would start to build these two, three, four, and sometimes five-story houses. The higher the house, the surer I had to be in placing the top cards! The lower floors had to be spaced just right to hold the upper floors. As the upper floors began to go into place my hand would begin to shake thinking this would be the house of all houses—the first twenty-story card house! Always in the back of my mind was how "weak it was" but those thoughts were replaced with "but look how fast I have gotten to the second and third floor!"

I inherited a house of cards from my father, one with no solid foundation. In the homes Doris and I were raised in, we faced the constant insecurity of starting over again fearing we might be erased! Nothing was for sure. Watching one parent do what *felt good* and seeing the other parent deal with the fallout of the other's decisions often left us caught in the middle of no man's land. We learned to live in a house of cards, never knowing when it would all fall down, wondering if we would have to start all over again not knowing where or who we might be living with.

I also learned to think that problems would simply take care of themselves. This is what I brought into my marriage. I believed Doris would be okay in time. She would come around. Things were really starting to happen at church, and by the way, I was able to glue the glass bed back together. [And they said it couldn't be done.]

Doris began having pain in her stomach! As the pain got worse it became necessary to take her into a doctor. I found myself sitting before a surgeon. He spoke to us in a hurried voice full of medical terminology that made little sense to me. But what I did pick up was that my wife could die in surgery and he wanted me to give my okay into a tape recorder microphone he placed in front of me. Full of apprehension, I gave him permission to go ahead with the surgery. Our first baby was lodged in Doris's fallopian tube and it was killing her!

As they rushed Doris off to surgery, I went to the waiting room and talked with God. After two hours, the doctor came out with our baby in a small dish. He said Doris was resting and to come back in the morning. As I drove home a couple of stories collapsed in our little card house.

Doris believed that God had judged her for the abortions she had as a younger woman. But when we got home she acted as if nothing was wrong. I could not understand how she could deal with such a tragedy so easily. It was like the stack fell but we were quickly rebuilding as if nothing ever happened. I didn't discuss her suppression because it came so natural to her, a dangerous character trait I would come to hate later on!

The doctor told us that the chances of Doris getting pregnant again were slim. Fortunately they were wrong. We probably could have named our second child Slim, because as he passed through the birth canal, the fetal distress monitor went crazy! Our little one was pulling away from his umbilical cord inside Doris! The doctors and nurses at Choc Hospital in Orange County, CA were terrific. They got our boy out just in time. Yes, he had a cone head, but he was "our little cone head" and we named him Gabriel. We were so close to a second big card collapse but this time our house stood firm with only a few shingles lost along the way. What a joy Gabriel brought into our home! Doris seemed truly happy as she took care of our baby.

Isn't it funny how life comes full of surprises. Before we knew it, "slim-two" was on her way! She was our "drive-thru" baby. The doctor told us that Doris would need to deliver this baby c-section because of Gabriel's hard delivery. We set a date and time, went in and came out with a baby (my version)! We brought our sweet Nicole Dawn Marie home. With any house of cards there is always an air of nervousness. When it was just the two of us if anything crashed or went wrong we could always start over, but you can't erase children and start over.

We thought we had learned another important principle; never build our house of cards *too* high. To fail in life is to be trapped in insecurity. All we knew is that we didn't want to live like our parents lived. Those raised in card houses constantly seek a normal, secure, life. When one marriage breaks surely there is someone else to marry. When one drug ceases to bring euphoria it's time to find stronger drugs. Always searching, never quite finding, always dissatisfied but hoping some new solution will appear; this is how so many live with their broken dreams. Card house living often leads only to bitterness and resentment towards those who seemingly live "the normal life."

We must remember our parents laid that first card for us and where they placed that card has a lot to do with the way we think now. In our case, God had to take us back to that first card and show us what it was leaning on.

Chapter 6

"Get Your Own Door Jam!"

Growing up in California the ground shakes every now and then. You learn as a child about the sounds of an earthquake. First there is no sound, the air is silent, birds stop singing, then the thought comes into your mind; something is not right. You think, "Wait! Be quiet." Something is going to happen. Of course the mind gets what it is waiting for. Suddenly, everything begins to move. This is when you start listening to the sounds, to know if it is the big one you have heard about all your life growing up in California. You wait for your parents to yell, "get under the door jam!" because most people in California think the door jam is the strongest place in the house. Growing up with an overweight brother and sister, while resembling a small spider monkey myself, had the big one ever hit; I would have had to run outside. The last words I would remember would be my brother and sister yelling at me "Get your own door jam!" as a telephone pole came down on my head.

When Gabriel was almost two years old, our world shook just like an earthquake and we went running for the door jams of our souls. We came home very tired from church and Doris had taken Nicole to bed with her. Gabriel was coming down with a fever and so I lay on the living room floor with him. We were all tired from a long day. Suddenly, I was awakened about two hours later by a tapping on my side. Thinking it was Doris because this is the way she woke me up, I turned toward the tapping and I found my son in a full-blown seizure. The tapping was his little hand hitting my side. He had stopped breathing and was turning blue. I jumped to my feet and picked up my son who was stiff as a board and ran into the bedroom yelling for Doris. She dialed 911 and Gabriel was taken off to the hospital. We thought we had lost him.

Gabriel had many tests to find out what was wrong with his body. He would suffer many seizures throughout his young life and we were powerless to stop them. After a spinal tap and many trips to the doctor we learned that Gabriel's seizures were triggered by the slightest fever. The fever would spike in a very short period of time triggering the seizures.

Not long after Gabriel's first seizure, Nicole began struggling to breathe. We took her to the doctors and found out that she was born with a flat voice box. When she breathed she chirped like a little bird. The doctor told us she might have to have a tube placed in her trachea until her voice box fully developed. He said that if we monitored her for a week or two and managed her breathing pattern there was a possibility of improvement. I found that when her breathing patterns were irregular, a slight nudge would bring her breathing back to normal. This kept Doris and I busy and very tired. I would take Gabriel and watch him and Doris would take Nicole to monitor her as we slept at night.

Once in a matter of days we took three trips to the emergency room. First we had to react to Gabriel's seizures, then to Nicole's breathing and finally for me when I acquired food poisoning from the hospital where Nicole was admitted. As if all of this was not stressful enough, my father died. Losing him was a big blow. Growing up my Dad was a source of fear and bitterness. But I had the joy of leading him to the Lord in his senior years and his life was transformed. In the process we enjoyed wonderful times together. Now he was gone.

On top of this entire trauma, our bills began to pile up. Early after having children, Doris became a stay-at-home mom. Because we only had one income we fell further behind in paying our rent and other bills. Along with my furniture job and serving as a full-time youth pastor, I took a job working at a pizza parlor.

I found during hard times all the things I saw and heard my parents do, set a pattern in my own thinking. When hard times hit your parents, what did they do? How did they learn to cope? What door jams did your family learn to run to for safety? What things in their minds were strong and safe? What coping mechanisms did you bring to your relationships, family and marriage?

Some people have family to step in and help when they encounter problems. They can handle the extra burdens. Others have nice bank accounts. Some folks rely on the government. Still others have a close friend who will go the extra mile to help them. But what we rely on can turn against us. Often people trying to help us can only see the outside of a problem and they judge it without fully understanding the situation. Often we can become so reliant on help from others that they become our proverbial "door jam." We deposit a trust in that help and that deposit is called our "soul" and many souls are deposited in all kinds of things and people. Boy what I believed and what my soul belonged to were two different things and this became very clear to me when these hard times hit.

In my head I knew GOD would take care of my family and me because His Bible told me so. But in the way of what should have been faith, was my own trust in myself to get through the trials. I was my own door jam. It's when we rely on our own solutions that we get into trouble. When things get too bad to handle many don't have the faith in God they need and when they find they cannot handle their struggles they walk away from Him.

When Jesus came to earth He said, "**I am the way, the truth, and the life. No one can come to the Father except through Me.**" (John 14:6) He made a clear declaration that He is the One in whom we can trust. When hard times hit I have to decide which way I should go and what I should do. What is the real reason for this experience? What is it saying to me and about me? What does life have for me now that this has happened? What will life be like?

I believe Jesus came to earth and walked the same life roads I walk. He purposed to show me a way through trials so that I could exit the other side without being so full of myself or wearing a victim-mentality in this mean world. I learned that my hard times had meaning. They were put there to change me, and I was going to be re-made like a house from the ground up, a house with no door jams.

Chapter 7

Why?

Why is that tiny word which describes volumes of our thought life. From the time life begins this word couples every problem we face. The first thing we think is "why." It seems like it shows up in our thoughts, right out of the womb! Have you ever looked into a baby's eyes after they are born? Their eyes seem to ask the question "why?" And when they begin to talk, it's the word that will wake us up in the morning, letting every one know they are alive! "Why mommy? Why daddy?" *Why* looms in front of us like the proverbial hot dog on a string just out of reach, as we spend the rest of our lives trying to catch it. As each question is answered another "Why?" takes it place. And so goes life. When we lose the questions I think we lose connection with our purpose here on earth, and when that happens we just exist.

Keeping our questions sincere is most important when we are looking for answers outside of our world. When the *why* question is properly used, it brings us back to our Creator, the One Who put us here. It fulfills the purpose for which it was designed. Asking God questions is what we call prayer.

Before I met Doris and before I knew whether God was even real, I hit that place where we all wind up sooner or later. I was asking questions like, "What is life all about?" "Why am I here?" I was looking for answers that could only come from someone bigger than me, bigger than humanity. I needed answers from One Who could look into the heart of things, know the motives, the essence and point of our existence, and here I sat with the biggest "why" question yet! The huge why that concerned His very existence and what He expected of me! "Don't ask it, it's a fool's question! Only a child asks things like that!" And then it hit me. The child's question is the most sincere thing we have left in this world, so I did it.

One day alone in my apartment, sick of living a life that was unfulfilled, I broke the rule of my polished intellect; I looked up to the ceiling and said with all the sincerity that I could muster "Whoever

You are up there, show me what to do?" And then I waited. I believed what I asked was honest, not knowing what was going to happen. It only took six or seven seconds before a knock at the door arrested my attention. I walked over and opened it to find a young woman standing there and she asked me if my roommate was home. I told her "No" and then she asked if I wanted to go to church with her, and I said "sure!" So I went and heard about the One Who instantly answered my ceiling prayer! I learned about what He thought about me. It was a bittersweet encounter!

I found out that God in heaven did in fact make us. I learned that He didn't just make us; He loved us, so much so that He sent His Son, Jesus Christ to live on earth among us. I learned that Jesus lived a perfect life. Incredibly, He was put to death by evil people who crucified Him on a cross—all in accordance with God's plan. When I understood *why* Jesus hung on that cross it changed my life! The *why* question brought me to the path I was to travel. I learned that God's expectation was that I would follow His Son, Jesus. When I admitted before Him my sins and determined to put my trust in Him through His Son, I answered the question as to why I existed.

As Doris and I struggled through Gabriel and Nicole's poor health, I spent long nights studying the Bible. I began to gain many answers to my questions. I read about people who had gone through worse things than I was going through. I realized that God's answers to me when they came would be the right ones just as His answers were right for those I read about in the Bible.

The youth group I was working with grew in a big way. As I taught them the things I hung onto in the Bible it became alive to them and to me! Those were fun years with the youth. Some of those kids went on to become pastors and teachers and missionaries. Then I saw the men in our church needing a chance to grow in their faith so we started a group for them, and it took off! Men's lives were changing and their wives noticed! It seemed as though whatever I got involved in turned to gold.

Jesus said He was the good Shepherd and we are His sheep. Unfortunately, I started to move ahead of the Shepherd and forgot that I was a sheep. We are to keep Him in front of us not push Him aside just because He is not moving fast enough. There's never a time when it is right for us to tell Him, "Thanks Jesus I can handle it from here!" The things I was doing started to reveal my fingerprints, not our Lord's.

Then one day, God threw a "Why?" on me. He said, "Why are you running ahead of me?" We know when God asks a question it's not because He doesn't know the answer. It's because we don't want to ask the question. *"Why am I running ahead?"* The answer was not good. Despite Doris' struggles, life revolved primarily around me and how I looked and what people were thinking about me! There I said it! I waited for some celestial hammer to come smashing everything down around me! But sometimes God doesn't completely smash things He takes the center and breaks it. In my case, His question to me broke my heart. I asked Him, "Why do I do this to you and to others?" I realized that my "me first" attitude had been a pattern in my life for too long, and I knew it! Why?

Chapter 8

"Check Out This Toolbox!"

In my line of work, the toolbox is a thing of pride because not much else is! Tim at work is the "go to" guy when it comes to toolboxes. He tries to fit everything in one box, which is quite a feat. He is always on the lookout for the perfect box for us. I believe the last one he found will not be topped unless someone finds one that can carry a small repair man and a chair so Tim can sit and watch him get his work done! Our current toolbox has more pockets then we have tools. When we go into a customer's home and open up this toolbox it looks like we know what we're doing.

There is nothing like a job well done. It happens in my line of work every now and then. My job is to repair furniture. Once I see the problem and conceive the solution the work begins. It's when I cannot see the problem or misdiagnose things that work really gets tough! This is how I looked at the problem in my heart of getting ahead of God. I could only see it from my view not God's view. I tried to change it the way I thought it would work. This made it worse.

    I came home from church one day thinking about Doris and the kids and things at church. The pastor and I were not getting along. Doris was wearing out from taking care of the kids with their special needs and trying to handle the pressure of being a "pastor's wife" with all the expectations that brings. My mom, whom I loved dearly, passed away at this time. I always liked talking to her. She had a way of making me feel everything was going to be okay. I would miss her encouragement with me on the go all the time trying to keep everything working.

    So as I sat there at home, I looked over and saw a tape I had wanted to watch. It was a story of a man's life with God and how he turned over the management of his life to God—something I had not done. I was used to determining my own course of actions so I could have some control. After I watched the film I started to think, "Why am I always seeing the outside of things?" My love is conditional. I only hang around people who believe what I believe." I felt our church was turning into a country club;

we were more into keeping people happy then in promoting their spiritual growth. I wanted at that moment to have the life that Jesus died on the cross for me to have. So I prayed, *"Dear Lord, I want to see people and life through your eyes. Change me!"*

I believe when it comes to working on us, God's toolbox is not that big. And in His box of tools is an instrument that is often misunderstood by those He uses it on. The tool I'm referring to is called *pain*. Pain does perfect and complete work. Our Lord does not use it on everyone but those He picks to endure pain rediscover what it means to walk the path of His making. They began to see life and the world with a whole different perspective.

About one month after I uttered that *"Change me"* prayer, I found myself returning things to people from church that I had borrowed, mostly to the pastor. I felt like I was leaving, but there was no signs pointing to this. Until the night Doris came to me telling me she could not sleep. This was repeated for about four nights and on the fifth night she came in and fell to the ground and yelled "I am going to hell help me!" I jumped up and held her. I could tell by just holding her something was leaving her and nothing in my toolbox was prepared for the challenge we were about to face.

Chapter 9

Rules Of The Game

I love sports and have been involved most of my life as a kid and as an adult. For me the rules are the challenge. They are what make the game *the game*! The key is playing within the rules and not breaking them. This must say a lot about me. Learning how to play is the hard part, but once that's over the fun begins. The rules frame the game like a picture creating the context by which we can compete. When players or a team design their game around cheating I just walk away. This thinking flows into my life off the field of play. I don't like people who cut in line, or who don't wave in appreciation when you let their car go in front of you. There are rules in life that some people don't want to obey. But when someone breaks those rules we say, "that's not fair!" On the playing field we yell "foul!" But what do we say when God breaks our rules? What do we do when God takes the frame that defines our life picture away and the rules change?

This is how I felt as the orderlies peeled my wives fingers off my arms, as I left her for her first night in a mental hospital. Who is going to call "foul" to God? Who's going to say, "It's not fair!" This time I could not just walk away when the rules were ignored. My white picket fence blew down, the weather got dark, the glass shattered, the clouds covered the rock face, the house of cards crashed and there was no door jams to run under. Why God? Why?

I came home from the hospital to a house with two little kids who wanted their mommy. Friends wanted to know what had happened. I felt like I went kicking and yelling into the grace of the Lord. This grace would come to be the new picture frame of my life. The boundaries of this new frame were so large that my old frame, the one I could selfishly control, the one where I arrogantly determined the rules of fair play was obliterated. This new frame was so large that anything could happen to my family or me. The first rule of this new frame was "You can't fix Doris."

Doris stayed three weeks in the hospital. Every day I tried to fix her by telling her over and over again that she was <u>not</u> going to hell. She only looked at me and heard words, which for her meant nothing. But that did not stop me. The rules inside my old frame said this should have not have happened and it will not happen! I gave God my life and this is what happens to those who serve him, those who keep the rules?

Two new friends showed up in my life—Anger and Bitterness. They kept trying to convince me that they could guide me through this new frame God created. But they were not the friends God wanted me hanging around. However, sometimes late at night when the answers were not coming fast enough, I would leave the back door open and by morning they would be sleeping on the couch only for me to chase them out again. They must have been smokers because it was hard to breathe when they were around.

At the end of the first week in the hospital, Doris started the "If this happens with me, and if this happens, then I will know I am not going to hell." So off I went to make things happen. One of the first things she made me do was go to the police and let them know where she was so they could come and arrest her for all the bad things she had done. She said it would prove to me how bad she was and this is why she was going to hell. I told her I would go to the police and have them write up a statement that said she was not wanted and there was no warrant out for her arrest. Then I could prove to her that she was wrong and was not going to hell.

As things would have it, when I went down to the police department to have them create an *easy little report*, the desk officer on duty was a Barney Fife-type (hyper man with too many questions). He wanted to know everything about Doris. I kept telling him that I knew there were no warrants for her arrest and if he could just write on the back of a police business card that she was not wanted how much it would help her (and me). Finally he did, and what he wrote was "To my understanding she is not wanted." Great! This did not go over well with Doris.

Doris sent me on another trip to one of the biggest churches in town. She said if the pastor would tell her she was not going to hell she would believe it. I could only get the assistant pastor to call her. As I went from one thing to another trying to show her she was not going to hell, they all failed. So I went back to talking to her, but this didn't work either, although it did save on gas since I didn't have to drive around. This hospital she was in was supposed to be a Christian-based, mental-health hospital and they were going to give me a discount on the price, because I was a pastor. I'm just giving some advice here. Whenever you hear discount and mental health put together in a sentence, don't buy it. The care was lacking and they could *not* help her.

Doris was transferred to another hospital that my insurance covered. But this hospital got her mind thinking in another way, away from God. Although the care was much better, I had to work hard to let them know not to take God out of the picture. To them this was amusing and they would let me know it from time to time. But this was my wife and they had to listen. Doris was not getting better, but for the first time she was not getting worse. She was in some deep, dark and hellish place. This is where she landed and stopped falling. It could not get any worse. The three-week journey was over. She was in hell.

Doris ran from a tidal wave most of her life, a huge wave of shame and fear. She tried to outrun it by being perfect so others could not see the "dirty little girl" but Doris finally tripped and the wave caught her. Now I know what left her that night when she first clung to me—HER HOPE.

The drive to the second hospital was a long one, about an hour and a half if there was no traffic. The drive home was longer because I would hope to see some change in her every time I visited only to see none. Sometimes I would take the kids with me to see her. But if she noticed them it was like they were someone else's kids. Fortunately Gabe and Nicole were too young at this point to know what was going through their mother's mind. It was not that she did not care for them or love them her mind just would not allow such privileges. This broke my heart one too many times and allowed me to venture into the heart of God and to what He calls unfair.

Chapter 10

"Just Fall!"

One time on my furniture job as I was walking out of a customer's home and after saying, "Have a nice day," the floor I was standing on gave way and down I went in to this dark basement. The only injuries I received were from trying to grab things on the way down to stop my fall. As I started to feel the future of Doris and my dreams giving way under my feet, depression started to come in and I wanted to grab hold of things to stop my fall. An old pastor friend told me, "Just fall. God will catch you when he thinks you have fallen enough." Little did I know God had a basement for me.

I watched as treatment after treatment and drug after drug failed Doris. The doctors switched to heavy medication and I knew they were trying their best to relieve her of her pain. I could tell that they were at their wits end in treating her. Doris started telling them that she wanted to go home. So they filled her with drugs and for the first time in six weeks Doris came home. What a homecoming! You see, the church we went to had people who had a hard time believing that a born-again Christian could have mental illness. So did I.

One thing I learned when Doris was in the hospital was that the mind has to draw a conclusion about everything it sees and hears and then files its conclusions. Others questioned whether Doris was really a Christian, something Doris wondered herself. So Doris tried to be born again repeatedly. This led me on a quest to find out what God had to say about mental illness. One of the first things I learned was that we are all mentally ill when it comes to God's way of thinking!

People switched their attention from Doris to me. The one thing I was holding onto was the fact that I was a pastor and with that position came a sense of status. Things were tough but I was still a pastor, a *somebody,* and this kept my head above water. Until my friends and pastor decided it was my turn to drown.

Without getting into the ugly details, I came home from work one night to find Doris holding a paper in her hand that said I was out of the ministry and some other rotten things about me. The pastor told people at church not to take any pastoral counsel from me. In effect he made us *persona non gratis*. Then he let my wife know what a rat he thought I was. You see I was going to go forward with some things he was doing that were hurting himself, his wife and the church. He knew he had to do some damage control with me and he had to act fast. The fact was I knew what he was doing.

I had been with him when he had done this to others. It didn't look so bad until I was the focus of his attention. Doris had only been out of the hospital for a week when this happened. That week, without saying anything to me, he went before the church to let them know that I was out of the ministry. Some called to ask what had happened and how Doris was doing, most didn't bother to call.

When you are in a position as a pastor where you have to tell people things they don't want to hear about themselves, some will love you for telling them the truth and some will despise you. Being young, I used little grace with my truth telling and this is why the calls were so few. This hurt, but it was true and now our church family was gone. It was like falling through the floor of the church and nothing was there to grab onto to stop my fast fall to the bottom. Now I was looking up from a dark basement with a mentally ill wife and two young children—a basement designed by God.

Chapter 11

Pulling Teeth

Most of us have a dentist story and here is mine. I had an impacted wisdom tooth that had gone wild and the roots took off in two different directions. It didn't show up very well on the x-rays so the doctor started off with just a simple extraction and about thirty minutes into it he said, "This is going to be a tough one." Now at this point, I was thinking the last thirty minutes were pretty tough. About one hour later with the doctor on my chest and my head feeling like it was going to come off before the tooth came out, I felt that tooth pop out with the doctor falling onto me saying "I got it" (like he just landed a trophy marlin), as he leaned on me to catch his breath.

This is how I felt after being removed from the ministry—like a big part of me was pulled out. What was left was sitting on my chest. There are times when God has to pull hard to remove things from our lives, things that we have been given freely only to wrap our selfish fingers around and control. God would have us live with an open palm with all the things He puts into our lives so that if He has to change things in our lives, He doesn't have to rip them out of our fingers.

It's good to check every now and then to look at what we are holding onto. What things do we feel we have to control all by ourselves that we don't want God's hand in because He may take them away or change them? God wants us to see life through His eyes and that this world is not the end of things only the beginning. We live sometimes like this is it! I have to fight and claw and wrap my arms around everything I have because someone or something is going to take it away from me. We live our lives in this mode and for the most part are *nice people* so long as no one comes between what is "ours" or challenges what we think.

Yes, I know I may have gotten under your skin as God has gotten under mine, but this is how He sees us and what He sees isn't pretty. We can't see it or don't want to see it, so we put ourselves around people and things that keep us blind. We stay away from the truth and people who can tell us the truth about God. Jesus did not die on a cross for robots. He died for the heart of the people who hate Him and don't want to hear about Him and could care less about what He has to say. Those who twisted His story and His words, these are some of the people He had in mind when He hung on that cross paying the price for the wrong that is in each one of us.

Sometimes it takes losing a tooth to see better the people God loves. The first thing God put in front of these new eyes was my wife. Doris blamed herself for all the things that were happening to us and tried to kill herself. She had to go back to the hospital where she remained suicidal. At times it seemed like I could see what it was that had a hold on her thinking but I remained unable to help her.

Doris went through a series of electro shock therapy. The doctor told me that this therapy had a 90% success rate. I remember this gave me new hope. Doris underwent the shocking and as I sat there with her after the treatment we would talk. It would be so hard watching her because she would come out of the treatment looking and feeling fine. We would talk like she had no care in the world. I would think this could be the one that works and our lives could finally start turning around, only to watch time and again a dark cloud descend on her thinking. I watched her try to fight and lose and plummet back into her hell. The doctor said to me that he could not give the treatment any more and that Doris was the 10%. He called me into his office at the hospital and talked to me about how I was doing and for the first time started to tell me that things were not looking good. He asked what my plans were for the future. I knew he was trying to ease my way into the fact that to keep thinking things were going to get better with Doris was wishful thinking and not based in reality. I thought he did a good job. Maybe not in the way he hoped but he helped me see what I was up against.

I was learning for the first time in all of this that the answers would be there when it was time. God was watching the seconds on this new clock I observed ticking. I don't think I was giving the doctors at the hospital the things they were waiting to see, like me getting on with my life. So they tried bombarding me with drastic words. They let me know that Doris was not getting better and the hope of her recovery was "slim to none." They had a place where she could be committed to that would take care of her for the rest of her life and they suggested it was time for me to get on with my own life.

You may be thinking right now this must have been a hard thing to hear, but it wasn't. The first thing I thought was it was God's way of giving me a way out because I had been at this for almost two years now. The doctors had all the papers ready for me to sign and off they would take Doris. So being the great Christian man that I am, I asked if I could go pray before I signed my wife's life away (knowing as they did, I would be right back to sign). As I went back and sat in the car, I started my prayer by thanking God for giving me a way out of this believing that Doris and I were now going to finish the rest of our lives on different paths. The kids were not asking for their mom anymore so maybe this was best for all of us. Maybe starting over wasn't a bad thing. Maybe it was time for the kids and me to head towards greener pastures and out of this dark gruesome valley.

I waited for God's answer. It came in a very simple way in my mind. I thought about all that I had been through with Doris, the birth of our children, the talks of our hopes and dreams for them. I remembered our lives together and most of all what we had been going through. Then I heard that strong, soft voice of our Lord saying, "Bring her home."

I went back in the hospital to let the doctors know my decision. They did not like the answer. They let

Hard Faith

me know what I was taking on and that they could no longer help me because I was turning away from their answers. Then they asked about my kids and how I was planning on taking care of them and my wife. I let them know all that I had been through up to this point had shown me I could do it. For the first time they agreed. I thanked them for all they did and in a way was going to miss them. They returned the same sentiment. As I loaded up all Doris' things to bring her home she showed me on her wrist where she had tried to cut herself the night before. I let her know that if she killed herself and she was thinking she would be going to hell that maybe killing herself was not a good idea. This stopped her from trying anymore. This way of communication with her I would come to find out was more for me to understand her, then for her to understand me. Here we were on our way home looking at the world a little bit different and me saying once again "What did I just do?"

Chapter 12

"Go to Hell!"

At my work, "Go to hell" is a popular phrase. The folks that say this don't really realize what they are saying. Nor did I before I became aware of what it meant. It means to damn someone to a place where people's teeth grind into their gums from the pain they are going through and wail from the torment of their minds—a condition that remains for all eternity. Maybe if you are using this phrase you will think carefully about it before you use it again.

The first year with Doris back at home was very hard. It seemed like everything that could go wrong went wrong. I went behind Doris fixing things one problem at a time. I took her off five of the seven drugs she was taking. The outpatient doctor was okay with this because she was just too drugged up for her safety and that of the kids.

The children were at school most of the day and I would be home right after they got out. Some days things got tight on time and I would get home later only to hear problems that Gabe and Nicole experienced or observed with Doris. It was heartbreaking to listen to them tell about something their mother had done. They loved their mom and at times understood her better then me. I just wanted the whole thing to be over with while they took life on one day at a time.

Once my son got into a fight because of something someone at school said about his mother. This is how it was in our family; we were all fighting for her. This bond made us close and gave us a heart for people who are misunderstood. It also at times caused us to keep everyone else away.

Doris would be home by herself most of the day and would spend that time crying a lot. All that Doris had gone through had taken a toll on her body and when we would go out and see people on the street from our old church they would avoid us. Some would tell me they just couldn't bear to see her. I could understand them because at times I found myself in the same place with people I didn't understand and what they were going through did not line up with my theology so I would have pity for them from afar.

Doris knew people were pulling away and looked at this as God's judgment on her. One time she set out to make me pull away also, thinking that if she could make me mad she would speed up God's plans for me to leave her and then she would be all alone. Believe me she was doing a good job of making me mad! Let me add a little background to this story.

I was worn out. I caught pneumonia and a missionary friend of ours fresh from the mission field left a parasite in our home that gave me a horrendous case of crabs (little bugs that bite in the worst places and cause unbelievable itching). I had broken out with hives because my nerves were frayed. My boss threatened me at work, because I was having a hard time keeping up with my workload. He said if I liked my job then I better start working a whole lot harder. My neighbor said I looked like Job. Now add Doris working me over while I am leaning on the bookcase that I have all my theology books on and in my mind I'm starting to boil. So I put my hand on top of the bookcase and I'm ready to pull the whole thing down and to say "The hell with everything." So I pray, "Lord help!" I don't know how it happened but a sudden peace came over me. I said to Doris, "Honey I am not mad at you." She started crying and told me she was trying to make me mad and that if I was mad than that meant God was mad at her. I told her I loved her and to *please* not do that again! As I walked away I thanked God for stopping me from letting my anger answer. This would be one of many times that He would call me to pray before I lost it.

There was a void between Doris and me. I tried to get her to see things the way I saw them. I tried pointing her to God only to have my advice fall on deaf ears. I was given a number from a pastor I knew to a counselor he knew. I thought I had tried them all but for some reason I gave this woman a call and she agreed to meet with Doris.

After two appointments she wanted me to sit in on one of their meetings. There I sat like so many times before, just waiting for the same stuff to come out of the counselor's mouth. But she turned to me after asking Doris some questions and asked "Dan where is Doris going?" I perked up and said, "Heaven!" She asked again, "Dan where is your wife going?" I looked at her like she didn't hear me and returned with "heaven." She looked at Doris and asked, "Where are you going?" Doris looked down. She knew the answer she was going to give was not what I wanted to hear. In her quiet voice she said "hell," all the while looking down. Then the counselor asked again, "Where is your wife going?"

I can't say how it happened, but it was like for the first time, I could see behind what Doris was thinking and that she was lost in an unfamiliar place and did not know the way out. Her ability to reason was gone, her mind had collapsed from the weight of her dark secrets and she was stuck down in the dark shaft in which her mind had fallen. Thoughts raced through my mind as I looked at Doris. I thought of all the time I had been looking for her, calling out to her to come to me and I could not hear her say, "Dan I can't." She did not want to drag me to her own dungeon.

I said, "Honey show me how to get there!" Then the counselor asked me, "Where is Doris at?" I said "Hell." She said, "Now you know where you need to go." The first thing that came into my mind was that I had just paid a woman eighty dollars an hour to tell me to go to hell! And for the first time in my life it was worth it!

Chapter 13

Everyone is Driving My Car

Do you remember your first car? Not the one you wound up with but the first one you wanted. The one you dreamed about and some said obsessed too much about. As you were out on the road it seemed to show up everywhere you looked. Parked on the side of the road, next to you in traffic, it seemed to show up everywhere. Then the heartache of heartaches you see one for sale and the price the owner wants gets you thinking, "If I could sell one of my major organs and float a loan maybe I could buy it." The car of my dreams was uncommon, it was a '39 Ford two-door that looked like a long bubble and was a beautiful candy, apple red. My parents diagnosed me as having a severe case of "car on the brain."

Part of Doris' condition was ruminating thoughts. She constantly had "hell on the brain." It seemed like everywhere she looked or whatever happened to her always somehow led her to conclude she was going to the place of everlasting torment! I didn't understand how she was drawing her conclusions. When Doris and I dated she told me about the car she dreamed of—a Volkswagen Bug that people turned into off-road machines. They called such cars *Baja Bugs*. I surmised that if I could get her to talk about other things besides hell maybe I could see why she was thinking the way she was. In a sense I needed to get into the front seat of her Baja Bug to see where she was going!

One night I found myself in the front seat of her Baja Bug. I couldn't sleep much because my mind took so long to shut off at night and this put me into a depression. At the time I did not know I was depressed because there was no time to dwell on my own condition. Depression is not something one can deny and just ignore. Often it firmly tells the mind, "I have had enough work I need rest." But I fought the notion of rest that left me with even less sleep than before. Depression then moves into a worse stage, which is to accentuate irrational thoughts. I began thinking things like "Just end it all so you can get some sleep and this bad nightmare you are in will all go away." So I began planning how I was going to end my life. It was so matter of fact like planning a vacation or figuring out how to fix a broken piece of furniture.

I figured I would drive my work van into a semi-truck on Pacific Coast Highway. People were frequently getting into accidents on this highway because there was no guardrail in the middle of this two-lane road and the speed limit was fifty-five miles per hour (mph). I wanted my death to look like an accident and not a suicide so my family would be taken care of through our insurance benefits. As I was lying in bed thinking out these details, my son Gabriel coughed in his sleep in the next room and this snapped me out of my morbid plotting.

Immediately I remembered I had a family to take care of and I realized I had gotten so centered on going each day and getting things done that I forgot my purpose as a husband and dad. So, I got on medicine that helped me get some sleep at night. This was the closest I came to understanding Doris. I also was aware that to get any closer would be unwise; I had to take care of myself. I began slipping out at night to run. This exercise was helpful and kept my mind from getting into traffic jams. Now that I had first-hand experience with depression I had somewhat of an idea when not to put too much pressure on Doris for fear it would only open her up for other hellish thoughts. As I look back, Jesus wanted me in the car, just not in the front seat, that was His place!

Chapter 14

Off Sides!

I have played soccer off and on for thirty years and in those many years I have met people from all over the world from different cultures and backgrounds. Many times after games I would talk with other players and I would get their worldview on things that could be quite eye opening! Soccer is a great means for building friendships. Aside from the competition, getting out on the soccer field and running around after a black and white ball is therapeutic for many players like myself. Accordingly, I try to play every week.

One of the challenges in soccer is playing according to the rules—something I mentioned earlier that is important to me! In particular there is an infraction called "off sides." Off sides in theory should be a simple foul to call for a referee, but we don't play with referees. We think they take away personal responsibility and slow the game down. So we leave the call to the last defensemen to make. Off sides calls tend to make people upset. Often the offensive player thinks the last defender made the wrong call. Sometimes the defender takes advantage and makes a subjective call to his own team's advantage. On many occasions the offensive player may be caught not paying attention and thus is embarrassed at being caught in the wrong position.

What makes soccer a study in human relations is watching what a player does after being called off sides. My theory is the worse a person's workweek or personal life happens to be, the more explosive the reaction is after getting accused of being off sides. In soccer not many goals are scored so when the player gets the ball, which he has worked so hard all game to get, and sees his chance to score taken away because of the foul call, his anger goes from embarrassment to yelling and in some cases walking off the field. Typically most just want the offended player to get over it and get on with playing unless the call happens to be personal. Suddenly, the one who moments before, just wanted the other player to get on with the game, wants everyone to hear his arguments as to why he was not off sides. Strange things happen when all these egos are out there competing. One after another we all get this foul called on us, one by one each one of us is embarrassed so we yell and make our foolish arguments. Of course, once our egos have been essentially neutered we go on to have a great game.

The Berg family was stuck in a dark valley where we got called "off sides" a lot by people who did not understand what we were going through and thought that embarrassing us would somehow help us. There were things in life that Doris and I just forgot to pay attention to—like the way we looked and acted. Because of the stress we were under, at times I felt like a homeless person just trying to survive. Unfortunately when I was embarrassed, yelling and arguing my side didn't do much for me.

Sometimes I met people who had their egos neutered by life and there was a common bond forged by mutual hardship. Other times I met people who drank too heavily from the cup of bitterness and they were constantly mad at everything. I had to fight from taking that poison many a time but it comes in so many flavors that there were moments when tasting it felt good. Sadly, poison can only kill or be spewed and I felt bad spewing.

God has a wonderful way of revealing our shortcomings. As I reflected on my wife's "taker" condition I began to think about Jesus. My Savior knew my own heart and my own condition yet He willingly went to the cross to deal with my sin. As I thought about His love for me, I realized, "who am I to be so frustrated with Doris just because she cannot give what I want or need!" Jesus knew my pain in its fullness but my pain did not come close to matching His. Therefore, He had every right to ask me to love Doris just as He loved me. Just like my friends and I had seen the worst of each other on the soccer field yet continued playing because we loved the game and saw past each other's shortcomings, so I needed to go on with my wife. I'm not saying it was easy. I needed hard faith because I often did not feel loved nor could I necessarily see God's love for me. All I knew was that the Bible promised, **"For God loved the world so much that He gave His one and only Son, so that everyone who believes in Him will not perish but have eternal life. God sent His Son into the world not to judge the world, but to save the world through Him."** (John 3:16,17)

I believe God really loves the world and sent Jesus to save us all—Doris, me, my children, you, and everyone else. Each day a lot of the decisions I make and will make lean on this belief called faith. Jesus said, **"I have told you all this so that you may have peace in Me. Here on earth you will have**

many trials and sorrows. But take heart, because I have overcome the world." (John 16:33) This world is made up like a soccer field full of competing lives each that carries his or her own stories. Often there are off sides calls that are improper or misunderstood and people get upset. But always there are people who are looking for fairness, who long for the right call to be made. God brought into our lives people who were not looking for us to be perfect just faithful to each other. These folks knew if Doris, the kids and I could make it together they could too. So our lives were more seen then heard, maybe not the way I wanted it to look, but I learned that this was okay. I started to live life seeing God as the answer not the question. People saw God at work in our lives when I could not. This was not God's problem it was mine. I was looking for things to get back to normal while God was working to deepen my faith that took me far away from normalcy. To stay married to Doris required steps of faith. Amazingly, mental illness and faith have something in common both are uncommon!

In order for my marriage to stay together my rules of behavior had to be grounded in faith. My faith could not expect that everything would turn out fine. There were many times when Doris made calls I did not like and I'm sure for her vice versa.

Rather, I had to believe God placed me in this place to act upon what I knew and not what I felt.

All my life I watched as selfish behavior destroyed relationships. Selfish behavior is fueled by the ego and it will do whatever it can to get what it wants unless it is put in check every day. I lived inside a body with physical needs. Daily I stepped out into a world that would gladly fulfill those needs. At times it was like walking through a minefield. In order to reduce the chance of me getting blown up some changes had to be made in the way I looked and acted to keep my sexual needs in check. I had to be satisfied with Doris and her condition. To let my mind wander would be the beginning of the end of my family so their lives had to mean more then mine.

I began to understand this was the language Doris could hear. My actions would either bring me closer or further away from her and this was quite a test to see what was in my heart. She would tell me she was going to hell many times a day and I would respond, "I am going with you." She would say, "No you are not." To which I would counter, "How do you know that? If I want to go to hell it's because you are there and that's where I believe God would want me to be." This conversation took on many, many forms but the message was the same.

I preached some of the greatest sermons I ever preached to my congregation—Doris. There were many times when I was amazed at what was coming out of my mouth. I began to see that my Lord had prepared me all my life to be here at this place with Doris; a place I never thought He would send me or any of His people. When I stopped fighting God's purpose and trying to change it I could see what He was doing. He was keeping me in this valley so I would know His holy ground. Psalm 23:4 says, "**Even when I walk through the darkest valley, I will not be afraid, for You are close beside me. Your rod and Your staff protect and comfort me**."

Holy ground can turn up anywhere. It's a place where God's people stop fighting where they are at and stop asking Him to take them out of their present surroundings. This holy ground can show up at the hospital bed or the gravesite or mental ward. It is where the dust of pain and confusion come to rest. It is where Jesus becomes Lord of my hurt as well as Lord my life. Just like in soccer, once my ego is put in check I am on the way to a great game. God called me to put my ego in check so I could see Him through the pain and accept the work He was doing in me. I'm so glad I did not walk off the field He had me on and leave my favorite player and miss the great lesson of trusting Him.

Chapter 15

Off Route

Whenever I went climbing I followed a guidebook that depicted the route up the rock and displayed points along the way where the hard parts of the climb were. Climbs were rated from 5.0 to 5.12. So when I looked at the guidebook the hardest part of the climb would have a rating like 5.7 so the route would be a 5.7 climb. Off I would go climbing knowing that the hardest part was a 5.7 and I already had experience with that degree of difficulty. I knew I would make it to the top so long as I stuck to the route.

There were times when I climbed when I accidentally got off route. Depending on how high up the rock I was had a lot to do with how I was going to get down. One time I was up about 950 feet on a

1000-foot climb and I was off route and the sun was going down. My climbing partner was looking to me to finish the climb because he had never been this high before. I went up into the over hang and when I got under it I reached over the top and started to feel for a hand hold. I found one, but it was not that good. I knew if I fell it was going to hurt! The rope would catch me eventually but at what cost to my body! My hands began to sweat and pull away from the rock. With 950 feet between the ground and me, I was running out of daylight!

After I brought Doris home from the hospital every morning I awoke feeling like I was off route. My wife and children looked to me to finish the climb. I must have asked myself a thousand times, "How did I get off route? What did I do to deserve this? Why me?" I had lived looking to the guidebook for every move I made in life.

A week came when the engine in my car blew up, I got sick and some people who I trusted were spreading hurtful rumors about Doris and me. I was not looking for trouble I was trying to hide yet still it sought me out! God was calling me off route just like he called Joseph in the Bible off route and David and Paul and many others. They didn't go looking for trouble, trouble found them! But God was using trouble to correct deficiencies in my life.

I learned along the way a profound lesson. What I thought was off route was exactly where God wanted me. He was calling me to be alone with Him spending time in His Guidebook. I came to find that it was not a book of rules as much as it was a book of life. The lower I climbed the richer the book got. You see I had already climbed mountaintops. Now God was teaching me to negotiate valleys!

So be truly glad. There is wonderful joy ahead, even though you have to endure many trials for a little while. These trials will show that your faith is genuine. It is being tested as fire tests and purifies gold — though your faith is far more precious than mere gold. So when your faith remains strong through many trials, it will bring you much praise and glory and honor on the day when Jesus Christ is revealed to the whole world. (1 Peter 1: 6-8)

Doris was in one of the deepest parts of the valley stuck in a cave. I was always climbing out of valleys not into them, so I needed to make some changes. I had to locate people experienced in valley climbing and I found them. People like Joni Eareckson Tada and C.H. Spurgeon were role models for me. Joni is a quadriplegic who through suffering has become a champion valley climber. In her books she writes about the greatest Valley Climber of all!

> **You must have the same attitude that Christ Jesus had. Though He was God, He did not think of equality with God as something to cling to. Instead, He gave up His divine privileges; He took the humble position of a slave and was born as a human being. When He appeared in human form, He humbled Himself in obedience to God and died a criminal's death on a cross. Therefore, God elevated Him to the place of highest honor and gave Him the name above all other names, that at the name of Jesus every knee should bow, in heaven and on earth and under the earth, and every tongue confess that Jesus Christ is Lord, to the glory of God the Father.** (Philippians 2: 5-11)

Climbing gear for valley climbers is much different than what I was used to using. First, I needed a harness called humility or I could not even begin to descend. Next I needed shoes of grace that handled the everyday mud valleys contain. My legalistic shoes that gripped rock faces were no good on muddy slopes. Then I needed a rope of faith unmade by human hands. My rope of self-confidence was meant to keep me from falling. God's rope of faith was meant to pull me to places I could not see.

Doris started to get up in the middle of the night and take off walking. I would not be able to find her, so I would have to wait and pray till she came home. She would return from her excursions and walk in the door barefooted. Many a time I had to remove glass from her feet. The valley was deep and I needed God to show me how to walk in it. I needed to know my first step.

One day Doris took off again but this time I was woken up by her crying and yelling and it was coming from outside in our front yard. As I looked out the front window I saw her sitting at the base of our tree holding onto it, crying and asking God not to send her to hell. As our neighbors looked on it was one of those moments in time when everything froze.

It's not like I hadn't helped Doris before! But this was one of those times when I had done something so long from *the hard place* it was like the weight of the world was on my shoulders. Every time I stepped forward to help Doris it seemed like everyone was watching me to see how I was going to handle her. All I could think about was being judged on how well I would do.

For as long as I could remember, "how I looked" was an ever-present concern for me. Up until this point in my life, it was always, "poor Dan with his mentally-ill wife." That tag kept me separated from my wife because it made me look more like a caretaker than Doris' husband. I knew that I had to identify with her before I could help her. I had seen it before among the elderly. For example, an old woman is hit with Alzheimer's disease. The husband deeply loves her and treats her as the bride he remembers he fell in love with so many years ago. The hugs and kisses still have the beautiful affection they once had. This is the love I always admired from afar but wanted nothing to do with because of how heart breaking it was to watch; we were too young for this.

God never calls us to live life according to our concept of time but according to His timeless concept of eternity. As I moved to the door looking out the window this verse of Scripture came into my mind. **"For husbands, this means love your wives, just as Christ loved the church. He gave up His life for her."** (Ephesians 5:25)

All my life I protected my reputation and sought to live according to my terms. I could take care of

Doris but to do so meant to give up my future plans, my goals and dreams—my climbing life. I knew this first move God was asking me to do meant I was committed to His kind of climbing. And His kind of climbing meant understanding and identifying with Doris, the woman He placed in my life to deepen my faith and teach us together about valley walking. If I continued to stand at the top of the valley too long with out taking the first step it would only lead to indecision after indecision. But the first step had to be the one God determined. I had gone through too much to get to this edge of the valley to turn back now. I knew from this point on I could not petition for sympathy or be concerned about what others felt because it was not about me anymore. Doris had to be the focus of my affection as the church was the focus of Christ's affection.

I walked outside the house and crossed the yard to the tree to which my wife clung. I pulled her fingers away from the bark and picked her up, put my arm around her and held her tight as I took my first step into the valley. It didn't matter any longer what the route was called, we were on God's path now.

Chapter 16

Time

We are all in subjection to it, no one can escape its calling. We plan our lives around it and hope it is kind to us. Some have too much, most have too little, but at some point all of us ask for more. Clocks plot its movement and history marks its passing. We will all fall victims to it, and are lost in it! Time doesn't change things but things change in time!

Doris' thinking had no time frame. For her, life was a constant thought of "It's too late the end has already come." She started to say things that showed me she was watching me descend into her valley. I began to ask her when she thought God was going to destroy us. She noticed that I was not leaving her. Repeatedly she asked me to go and just get on with *my* life. I let her know she *was* my life and if God was going to destroy her He would have to destroy me. One of the beautiful things about time is that it allows us to build trust. Doris begin to realize that my words were in line with my actions. We had been at this eight long years and I knew I had to keep showing her God's love.

Because Doris was abused she had a monumental problem in accepting or even understanding love. People she thought she could trust, abused and raped her all the while telling her they loved her. Those early feelings that she was told were love were not love at all, but a selfish power taking control of her and scaring her to the point of submission and then treating her nicely so long as she kept submitting. This is what she was told was love. In fact their words and actions came from selfish, evil lust. They scared Doris into submission while they traumatized her beyond reason. Consequently, Doris had a difficult time believing in the reality of love or that it could truly last. The thought of trying to find real love coupled with the possibility of losing it was just too painful for her to go through. So she either held my love at arms length or extinguished it by smothering me. Either way, she often ended up jeopardizing the very thing she coveted—my love.

To help Doris, I frequently told her that we had made it this far and we were still together. She knew this to be true and had no answer. I began reading two verses from the Bible to her every morning. **"The faithful love of the Lord never ends! His mercies never cease. Great is His faithfulness; His mercies begin afresh each morning**." (Lamentations 3; 22, 23)

I told Doris that it was because of God's mercy that we were not destroyed. God was patiently waiting for her to understand this and see His mercies as fresh each day. Trying to help her believe this was like turning around the Queen Mary cruise liner in the Santa Ana River! If you have ever been to Santa Ana California, you know the river is not that wide and the water is pretty shallow. Slowly we had to inch her mind to moving in the right direction. Sometimes we went backwards and sometimes we inched forward always working to move in the right direction.

Chapter 17

Choosing Miracles

"Miracles don't happen in our day," is what the agnostic scientist says. For him there is an answer for everything as he stands on a planet that is unlike any other planet in the known universe. "Miracles happen every day!" is what the veteran delivery room doctor says. What is the difference between these two views? One man sees miracles as nothing more than cause and effect; the other sees the handiwork of God.

Like the agnostic scientist, I saw miracles as everyday events that were no big deal as both a nonbeliever and to my shame, as a believer. I remember when Gabriel was about three years old he found out how fast he could run and so he ran everywhere and at times in to everything! One day we had some friends over and Gabriel was showing us how fast he could go. Bless his little heart he ran right into the corner of the wall. We all jumped up as he hit the floor. When we reached him we saw a growing knot on his head. Doris ran for ice. She got the ice wrapped in a towel and on his head in seconds only to hear Gabriel yell, "I can't see!" Our hearts sank as our thoughts raced. Doris removed the towel full of ice so we could examine his eyes. Instantly he yelled, "I can see!" We were all amazed at the instant miracle, only to find that the towel full of ice had covered his eyes. Miracles are everywhere but our intellect discounts them. As quickly as we found the cure to our son's blindness we discounted the miracle of his sight.

Doris needed miracles and I was losing faith that they could happen. I needed the eyes of the doctor. I needed to appreciate the ones that had taken us this far. Sometimes God gift-wraps miracles. One day Doris and I were talking outside. Desperately she was trying to understand God's love for her. I could see the strain on her face as she tried to figure this out. As she was standing there a string of bows fell out of the sky and landed on her shoulder. They scared her at first. But as she pulled them off she noticed an attached card. On it were three profound words, "Jesus LOVES you." She burst into tears, totally overwhelmed by this amazing miracle. This was one of several distinct events, which convinced Doris that God loved her, and had not given up on her. Now her question was, "So why have You not given up on me?"

My job situation began improving. The furniture company I worked for gave me positions with more responsibility. I was asked if I wanted to move to Oregon. This to me looked like a new beginning and as I prayed about it, there was no doubt this is what God wanted us to do. I was looking for a new beginning. I was led through a friend who worked at Calvary Chapel to contact someone he knew who lived in Oregon. This man, Larry Loge, was a realtor and a brother-in-Christ. Larry found an apartment for us. It just seemed as if God put all the pieces in place for us to move.

Soon the big day to move came. As we left the driveway for the thousand-mile drive for Oregon our little truck was loaded down with as much as it could carry and then some! Doris didn't show much emotion but the kids and I were pretty excited. We were driving to a place where no one knew us. We could finally get a fresh start.

Gradually, I thought Doris was relaxing and adapting to our new surroundings. Larry invited us to his church. Our first Sunday there the people took us in with open arms. It was so good to feel loved again. But all was not better quite yet. Doris felt overwhelmed by all the changes. She stopped eating and dropped below a hundred pounds. I had to put her back in the hospital. She so much wanted to be a part of this new beginning with us but it took more trust then she possessed.

I let her know we were waiting for her and would continue to wait until she was ready. A week before Christmas the doctor told me she could come home for two days. On Christmas Eve while I was on my way to pick her up, I prayed and asked the Lord as I had so many times before, to heal her. I pulled the car over and instead of asking my Father in heaven to heal her; I asked if we could just have a good Christmas. So many Decembers were filled with painful memories because Doris seemed to get worse around Christmas. *"Please God, give us a great Christmas together."*

I met my wife at the hospital and although I couldn't put my finger on it, there was a subtle difference in Doris. Not until I got home did I recognize what had happened. Doris had fallen in love with her children again! She made them little toys in the hospital and I could tell that she put a lot of care into them. The kids loved them.

Doris found that place that only God could lead her to—that place where all people who come to know Jesus eventually must pass. This is the place where trust and faith come together. Suddenly we understand and believe that when Jesus hung on the cross, He was there not only for the sin we have committed but also for the sins committed against us. Doris realized that her Savior covered all the evil she suffered. She found her new beginning.

The mercies of the Lord began afresh and new for Doris. To this day she keeps this truth in front of her each morning. Jesus dealt with all the bad things that happened to her and that may happen to her. No longer would her past haunt her because in Christ she truly became a new person. He put each new day in front of her and said, "Walk!"

God answered my prayer about how to love someone, by giving me a woman who did not know what love was. I held her through the storms and descended into her valley of fear to find the cave in which she hid. But I could not bring her out. Only God could do that. And in His awesome grace that is exactly what He did. He helped us through the valley. Doris was back!!!!!!!

Chapter 18

Paper Ham

Growing up we did not have much money. My dad left our family when I was four and so my mom had to work. My mother did not come from an impoverished background. Therefore it was hard for her to watch us cut cardboard out to put in our shoes to cover the holes. We experienced hard times but as a kid I didn't really know this. After all, kids adapt and make the best of what they have. I do remember that my mother was often sad. I'm sure looking back now that this had to do with her bearing the brunt of my father's poor choices. I also remember that my siblings and I believed it was our job to make her laugh.

My brother and sister are some of the funniest people I know. I believe their humor came from this time in our life. I always tried to be funny too so I could contribute to making my mom laugh. Perhaps my best moment was the time we were just about out of food. All we had were bread crusts and mayonnaise. My mom was miserable that we had nothing to put on the mayonnaise. So I went out and found a magazine with a picture of a piece of ham. I cut the picture out and placed it in on our sandwich looking for a big laugh. I said, "Look Mom! We have ham! She looked at the sandwich and then at me but she didn't laugh, she burst into tears!

The way we look at life largely has to do with our experiences growing up. If we grew up in a safe environment, then it is much easier to be trusting in people and to feel safe. If we grew up in an unsettled, turbulent setting, then it is much harder to trust people. The way we look at death is very similar to how we understand life. Some people have no concept of death because it is so foreign to them. For others, death is an everyday event. Despite our background and understanding, God still continues to work to accomplish His purposes.

I have learned that when I expect God to work in my life the same way He works in others' lives, I make a big mistake. The Bible was written for all people, in all stages of life and backgrounds. When I read the Bible I begin to understand that God's realm and way of viewing things is much different than my own. Sometimes it takes a lifetime to really understand what He is doing. Sometimes even a lifetime is not enough—for everything God does is not necessarily understandable.

I had my way of fixing Doris and God had his way. Guess whose way needed to change? Many times I felt my Heavenly Father was unfair but as I look back on this adventure I see He had a pretty hard heart to work with and all that happened to me was necessary. In order for me to experience peace and truly grow in my relationship with the Lord, I needed to yield to His will.

Shortly after Doris came home from the hospital she experienced what was truly a mountain top event. She truly recognized that Jesus would never leave her. Now, armed with that truth, she was ready to minister to people living in the valley. She told me, "I need to reach out to people." One day I came home from work to discover a big surprise. Doris climbed down the mountain we were enjoying to find a job. The very first place she visited hired her.

For eight long years we hated living in the valley. God brought us through that period and gave us eight more years and counting in which Doris has ministered to countless people. Gabriel, Nicole and I believe she knows practically everyone in our city and the surrounding cities. At the rate she meets people soon she'll know everyone in the country! If you don't know my wife yet, just wait, you will!

My kids have turned out to be as funny as my brother and sister. They are quite adept at making their mom laugh a lot! People have actually come over to our house to let us know they could hear us laughing as they walked around the corner of our street. To see Doris laugh is one of those things you just have to sit back and watch, there are no words to describe it. Sure life is not always easy. We still have setbacks and days that we wish were forgotten. But what we have gone through leaves us grateful for the blessings God provides.

Gabriel and Nicole are off serving their country in the Marine Corps. Doris' personality is like a cup of warm soup on a cold day to everyone she meets. She is living proof that God never leaves us or forsakes us. I have learned that God completes the pain of His children with His glory. There is <u>so</u> much to look forward to in following after Him.

I'm still fixing furniture. As I drive around in my van I can't stop thinking of all we went through. I meditate on the truth that despite all my uncertainties, God never left us. He was not there in the way I wanted Him to be. He was there the way He should be; giving me the thing I always wanted,

Hard faith!

Hard Faith

On a cold winter night where the rain danced with wind
    the forecast could only stay dreary,
He walked through the door and kissed his dear wife
    and they shared the day that expired.
His ritual was steady he headed to bed
    surrendered his body to rest
But sleep seldom comes to a mind in a maze
    searching a way from the fire.

Hours passed by what seemed eons of time
    when he woke in a place called Illumine
In a house with no roof with the sun shining bright
    and the birds singing songs with the angels.
He looked to the floor that was covered with glass
    broken in pieces all jagged
He noticed the windows were empty and bare
    and that's when He spotted the Savior.

Hard Faith

The power of faith is a powerful thing
I won't stumble for long when I sit on Your wings.
I look up to find You and ask You for strength
To live in a way that brings glory to You.

His eyes were as blue as the deep ocean water
    His face bore the lines of a sage
His hair was as white as the robe that adorned him
    when he walked as a King through the door.
Without saying a word He spoke in my mind
    and I knelt down and picked up a shard
What I saw as I looked through that uneven piece
    brought tears to the depths of my soul.

Again and again he told me to pick up
    the stained glass that littered the floor
Each piece like a movie unfolded a view
    of a pain that she had endured.
The trauma grew worse and I begged him to stop
    but He urged me to keep going on
Her past like a fighter kept beating my head
    and that's when I looked at the panes.

Every piece of my wife that was shattered by evil
    He'd taken and fit in the frames
'Til the holes in the walls became filled like a gallery
    and the pictures they made were astounding.

His face took the place of her unending sorrow
    His peace made each piece a whole
His grace made the difference His mercy was awesome
    and I was amazed by it all.

But He wasn't finished this One Who is timeless
    He took the last shard from my hand.
He placed it inside the hole in His wrist
    and covered it there with my palm.
Every question I wrestled every doubt I embraced
    was answered by His perfect love
I woke up rested with His voice resounding,
    "My son, your hard faith has won."

The power of faith is a powerful thing
I won't stumble for long when I sit on Your wings.
I look up to find You and ask You for strength
To live in a way that brings glory to You.

©2006 Daniel L. York **First Cause** ARR
Dedicated to Dan and Doris Berg

For questions or comments regarding **Hard Faith**, please e-mail the author at: berg_family@sterling.net or contact us at **First Cause**, http://www.first-cause.org/bookstore/index.html. If you would like to purchase more copies of this book, you can order directly by calling us at: 1-866-909-BOOK (2665) toll-free.

About the Author

Daniel Berg was born on February 25, 1957 in Los Angeles, California. He grew up in Southern California with one brother and sister. Most of Dan's early childhood was spent without a father. In high school he became active playing soccer. His skills and knowledge of the game were such that he went on to coach high school and college soccer as well as playing on a semi-professional team. Dan became a follower of Jesus at the age of twenty-two. Four years later he began serving as a youth pastor with a Calvary Chapel in Orange County. Currently he works as a furniture repairman throughout Oregon and Washington. Dan continues to minister as both an elder and a teacher of God's Word. He and his wife Doris enjoy fishing, reading and hiking.

About the Cover

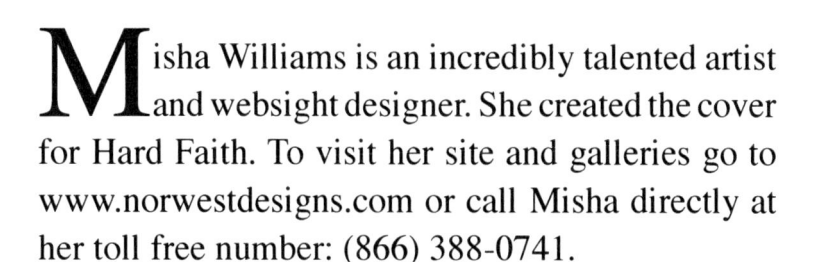

Misha Williams is an incredibly talented artist and websight designer. She created the cover for Hard Faith. To visit her site and galleries go to www.norwestdesigns.com or call Misha directly at her toll free number: (866) 388-0741.

CPSIA information can be obtained at www.ICGtesting.com
Printed in the USA
LVOW08*2135030614

388500LV00004B/32/A